The Gifts of Pain

"31 Uplifting Stories to Give You Comfort and Help You Cultivate Wisdom in Adversity"

By 31 diverse authors who courageously share their painful stories and the tools that helped them turn them into gifts

Compiled by

Visionary Author Elayna Fernández

The Gifts of Pain
31 Uplifting Stories to Give You Comfort and Help You Cultivate Wisdom in Adversity

Compiled by Elayna Fernández

Content Warning: The stories in this book include sexual violence, familial violence, chronic disease, discrimination, self-harming behaviors, abortion, terminal illness, death, eating disorders, suicide, mental illness, bullying, poverty, gun violence, shame, addiction and substance misuse, autism, pornography, sexual harassment, exploitation and assault in the workplace, imprisonment, and other content types that may be upsetting or triggering.

If you or someone you know is struggling or in crisis, help is available.
Call or text 988 or chat at 988lifeline.org.

Developmental editing by Elayna Fernández
Copyediting by Eleyrin Fernández
Published by thePositiveMOM.com

To the younger versions of yourself.
May they be proud to know you've grown into someone
who would have comforted and protected them.

Table of Contents

From Pain to Gift
by Elayna Fernández

As a professional speaker for almost two decades, I've been hired and sponsored by both for profit and non-profit organizations nationally and internationally to share my stories and teach the art and science of storytelling.

One of my most requested talks is about what I call the alchemy of pain. This concept inspired The Gifts of Pain series, and I'm so grateful you're reading the third book!

Although I am only an alchemist figuratively, I want to share with you why this analogy works so well. Alchemy is not only a method of transformation – a transmutation of something basic into something superior and far more valuable – its process is an analogy to the hardships we endure in this human experience.

The stage of *Calcination* symbolizes the purifying fire that destroys something in us and turns it into ashes. *Dissolution* is a metaphor for how those ashes stir our souls. As Maharishi Mahesh Yogi, the creator of Transcendental Meditation (TM), would say:

"Love will cause anything unlike itself to come up to be healed."

Separation happens when our emotions start to settle and we are able to discern that which we must let go of and that which we must treasure.

In *Conjunction*, we start to use our new awareness to create a new reality. In *Fermentation*, we align with the truth we discovered about ourselves.

Then comes *Distillation,* a time for refining and discarding any impure residues that might remain from what was burned.

And finally, *Coagulation,* where we find the gold - the pure light of love, joy, peace, and freedom.

As you immerse yourself in this 31-day journey, there might be a lot that comes up to be burned – and healed. Remember that you are not alone, dear pain alchemist, and your adversity is not your destiny.

Elayna

"Your adversity is not your destiny."

ELAYNA FERNÁNDEZ

From Defeat to Triumph
by Lesia Davidson

I found myself trapped in a dark box, unable to escape. Huddled in the school closet one day, I heard a loud grumbling voice. I shivered as I put my head between my legs and continued to sob. The door squeaked as it slowly opened.

The voice boomed.

"What you doin' in here?"

It was Tanya. We had become friends with her schoolwork, and every day, we would meet to study.

"Janet pickin' on me," I answered.

"Oh-ho-ho, really?" she said in a deep growl, flabbergasted that Janet didn't heed her initial warning to leave me alone.

Janet was 6' tall and her body was as huge as a heavy grey elephant. At 4'8 in the 5th grade, I saw everyone as giants.

Tanya quickly grabbed my wrist and sped down the hallway while my limp body flailed from side to side. We came to an abrupt halt. I nearly fell face-first to the floor when my fall was interrupted by her oversized leg. Phew! A loud yelling was exchanged, and I heard, "Pick on somebody your own size. Pick on me."

Janet, the giant bully, walked away, her face turning beet red as the entire school began to cheer Tanya, the gentle giant. The protection of my guardian angel continued to cover me.

As a teacher for 23 years, I taught my students that a guardian angel will appear when life knocks you to the ground. You won't just try to get up you get up, shake yourself off, and charge onward. I share these lessons with the children in my reading readiness programs.

I invite you to remember the guardian angels in your life and to be a guardian angel for others. Show someone love, kindness, peace, empathy, and compassion, and execute your guardian angel power.

Your Turn

Pause for a moment. Close your eyes and recall an instance when you faced a challenge or felt vulnerable.

Who or what helped you through that moment? Perhaps it was a friend, family member, or even your own inner strength. Reflect on it below:

_____

_____

_____

_____

_____

Share a simple act of kindness you plan to do. How can you be a "guardian angel" in someone else's life, whether by standing up for them, offering support, or creating a welcoming environment?

_____

_____

_____

_____

_____

"Your guardian angel will appear,
you will get up, shake yourself off,
and charge onward."

LESIA DAVIDSON

From Suffering to Vitality
by Kris Hapgood

After 20 years as a nurse, I took heavy painkillers just to function. I was in denial about how my physical chronic severe pain and brain fog impacted me at work. I felt like I was 100 years old and my body was failing me. Did I have to live like this for the rest of my life?

One day, my daughter came to the house: "Mom, I am so concerned about your wellbeing. I'm bringing you a natural alternative that will help you."

As she applied the blue cream with essential oils, I was skeptical. Within a few days, I felt a sense of relief from the pain I didn't think was possible. I started to feel whole and in control of my wellness and my life. It was shocking to see the evidence-based research documenting how our bodies can heal themselves.

Many of my medical colleagues didn't acknowledge that the "medical system" was misleading people or harming them. Patients don't always have *all* of the information or don't make true informed decisions.

I wasn't allowed to speak to patients about options of natural treatment plans or living proactively.

God called me to use my wisdom and experience to empower others to make better-informed decisions about their health. I quit my nursing career and started my own wellness business.

I now work directly with people to resolve health/wellness issues by addressing the root causes rather than treating the symptoms. Enlightened with freedom from the medical status quo, they transform their lives through education and advocating for themselves.

I invite you to advocate for yourself, become healthier, and live to the fullest with vitality and strength.

Your Turn

What would help you feel more vitality, strength, and in control of your health?

_____

_____

_____

_____

How can you advocate for yourself and your wellness?

_____

_____

_____

_____

What would a "perfect day" look like to you? How would it make you feel?

_____

_____

_____

_____

"Live to the fullest with vitality and strength."

KRIS HAPGOOD

From Desisting to Existing
by Kaleigh J. Urbanek

I hated that he had the power to take this away from us. There was nothing we could do to stop him. He tried covering it up: "We need to make room for the boys. It's *tradition.*"

Our pastor, "Father C.," announced that females would no longer be allowed to serve at any future masses. This felt like a slap in the face to me and every woman before me who had gone to my school. Initially, I was confused. I had heard people experiencing gender discrimination, but I never thought it would happen to us.

I felt helpless, mourning the loss of my right to serve while my fate lay in the hands of our merciless pastor, shaking our rights like dice in the hand blessed by God.

Word spread fast. Nobody was happy. I heard the angry whispers of other students and the disheartened voices of teachers that were usually so bright in the mornings. A male student even told the pastor: "I'm disgusted by your decision."

Seeing the collective outrage reminded me that I have the power to stand up for the rights that belong to me and others. I mobilized my friends by bringing inspiration for protests and protest-like actions. I made buttons, posters, and poems to persuade others to join our cause and join our efforts.

To our surprise, the following week, our pastor gave a speech, apologized for his actions, and reinstated the rights of females to serve at mass.

Since then, my mission has been to encourage other young adults to consider using their voices through peaceful protests. Peaceful protests can be effective, easy, and free, so it doesn't cost anything to spark your movement.

You too, can make your voice and opinions known, to create justice and equality for everyone.

Your Turn

Now, it's your turn to make an impact on injustice.

1. Notice some injustices that happen around you. Is there something in your life or community that unfairly undermines you or some other group of people?

    (For example, unfair dress code, unjust treatment, inaccessibility due to the negligence of an authority figure, etc.). Write about it below.

    _____

    _____

    _____

2. Why are these rights important to protect?

    _____

    _____

    _____

3. Why are these rights important to you?

    _____

    _____

    _____

4. Who else supports the rights that you believe in? Write about their impact below:

    _____

    _____

    _____

5. What actions can you take to protect the rights you deserve and make your voice heard? (For example, peaceful protests, boycotts, spreading awareness, online petitions, message marches, joining activist groups, etc.) Write about it below:

    _____

    _____

    _____

"You have the power to stand up for the rights that belong to you and others."

KALEIGH URBANEK

From Losing to Loving
by Sharmeen Yousaf

My eyes were half-open as I checked the time on my phone after a 14-hour flight when a phone notification popped up: "Fareena has passed away." The words hit me like a punch. This can't be! I was supposed to hug her in two hours!

My younger cousin, who was like a sister to me, was gone. She loved everyone selflessly and had been there for me when I needed it most. I had hoped to catch up with her and hug her when I arrived. Now, I would never tell her how much I loved her, what she meant to me, and the difference she made.

I realized I had told myself I was too busy with life to recognize the importance of a real connection. This regret weighed heavily on me and taught me to express my love and gratitude through a text, letter, or call while I can.

To honor Fareena, I began to follow her example, reminding people to cherish their present relationships. I blog, speak on stages, and write books, teaching my audiences to embrace and express their feelings unconditionally. It has become my mission to teach others not just to say "I love you" but to go deeper, describing the small gestures that made a difference. Your kind words could be all someone needs to get through their day - and even have a lasting impact. Fareena's last words: "You are my role model," will live with me forever.

In today's world, it's easier than ever to connect. Take a moment to think about someone who has made a positive impact on your life, no matter how small. Decide you will tell them they are missed, you are thinking of them, or their kindness made you smile. Let's create a movement of gratitude and love.

Your Turn

Think about moments when someone made you feel loved. Write their name below.

_____

_____

_____

_____

What is a memory you share with that person that puts a smile on your face?

_____

_____

_____

_____

Now, reach out to them. Send a quick message to someone who made you feel good and let them know how much that moment means to you. Thank them before it's too late. It's a simple act that can brighten both your day and theirs.

Write down how it felt below:

_____

_____

_____

_____

"You are missed with love."

SHARMEEN YOUSAF

From Broken-hearted to Beloved
by Dawn Richard

I cried myself to sleep like I had hundreds of times during my 27-year marriage. What was wrong with me? Regardless of how much I sacrificed my needs and happiness for him and the kids, he didn't treat me with loving kindness or respect. It was never enough. *I* wasn't enough.

As a Licensed Professional Counselor, I helped many couples heal their marriages, yet I couldn't fix my own. I felt powerless, stuck, and unworthy of receiving the love I desired.

The next morning at the airport, I pulled my flight attendant's suitcase down the busy terminal, smiling despite how I felt. I suddenly saw a vision of the Virgin Mary, who told me, "You know what you need to do. Everything is going to be okay." At that moment, I realized I couldn't fix him or my marriage. I had to save myself. Our marriage was not the example of love I wanted for myself or my kids.

That's when I discovered the 3 Rs to heal any relationship.

1. **Release the past**. "Feel to Heal." We must allow ourselves to grieve for our lost hopes and dreams and let go of anger, resentment, and sadness. Forgive ourselves and others. Set ourselves free from guilt, shame, and judgment.
2. **Restore your heart**. We feel more peace and joy when we develop compassion, self-love, and acceptance.
3. **Recreate your life**. We discover our true selves and follow our dreams. We allow ourselves to experience more fun, freedom, and fulfillment.

This discovery led me to speak, teach, and offer programs to help people heal heartbreak and love again, just like I have.

As you follow the 3 Rs, you will attract healthy and fulfilling relationships, starting with yourself. Love yourself deeply and become your own Beloved. You are worthy of love!

Your Turn

Use these questions to start your healing journey.

1. **Release the past**: What do you need to let go of? Who do you need to forgive?

    _____

    _____

    _____

    _____

2. **Restore your heart**: What qualities do you judge in yourself that you're willing to love and accept? What qualities do you already admire in yourself?

    _____

    _____

    _____

    _____

3. **Recreate your life**: What kind of new life and relationship(s) would you like to create?

    _____

    _____

    _____

    _____

*"Love yourself deeply and become
your own Beloved."*

DAWN RICHARD

From Pain to Purpose
by Uzi Makhdoom

I felt conflicted when I heard my mom say those words: "You were abused by your nanny when you were only 1 year old." We went back to house cleaning and cooking, but she didn't say how or why it happened.

I was numb as I reflected on my 18 years of life: losing my grandparents, uncles, and aunts at 12, and experiencing bullying and discrimination at school, which started when I was 15. I told myself I didn't care and decided that I would move on with my life.

Throughout this time, because of budget cuts at school, I kept getting a different counselor, and I hated starting over every year—like a CD player on repeat. At 18, I spiraled out so badly right before graduation that I saw an out-of-school therapist and ended up being diagnosed with poor mental health.

It was then that I realized that bullying is common and I'm not the only one. I also found the voice and power to stand up for myself. I learned I matter.

That's when I started to use my story as a healing tool, so it could be someone else's survival guide, helping them heal, and showing them that things get better.

I'm now a mental health advocate, anti-bullying and body positivity advocate, vocal as an activist and content creator.

In 2021, I founded the Mental Health Alliance Network, and through my podcast and vlog, I share my story and other people's stories, as well as resources for times of crisis.

I'm still facing losses as I finish college, but I thrive as I continue to live life authentically.

I invite you to reflect, learn, and explore yourself and your mental health, and proudly and authentically share your story, so you can heal and help others.

Your Turn

1. How are you taking care of your mental health?

   _____
   _____
   _____
   _____

2. Have you reached out for help? Why/why not?

   _____
   _____
   _____
   _____

3. What are some healthy coping mechanisms you can adopt to improve your mental health?

   _____
   _____
   _____
   _____

"Find the voice and power to stand up for yourself. You matter."

UZI MAKHDOOM

From Darkness to Radiance
by Nelanthini Rajesan

I sat in the car, tears streaming down my face, grappling with the unbearable question of why. I had just spoken to her a few months ago, and everything seemed fine. Now I'm reading her suicide letter, trying to put all the pieces together to answer the question: "Why her?"

The words seemed to leap off the page. Was my friend telling my story back to me? Five years before, I almost fell to the same fate. It was at that moment I realized that we were both chasing the endless pursuit of perfection and losing ourselves in the process.

This wake-up call prompted me to focus on the aspects of my identity that felt truly authentic. I chose to retreat into solitude, diving deep into meditation, journaling, and self-exploration.

It was during this time that I realized I had silenced my inner voice for years, becoming an empty shell by doing what was "right" according to others, instead of what I truly wanted. It was time to finally set her free. This journey revealed the essential tools and actions needed to rediscover oneself and ignite a personal rebirth.

I integrate these radiance tools into my daily life and share them with others, empowering them to transform their own lives for the better. We can all feel a new ignited passion for life and unlock a new level of freedom to live our lives the way we want. Through keynote talks and coaching programs, I am committed to helping women break free of limiting beliefs and live a life that is full of radiance and authenticity.

I invite you to start journaling and meditation to reflect on what societal expectations are holding you captive in the shadows and start living life on your own terms.

Your Turn

What societal expectations do you feel pressured to conform to? How do they impact your self-esteem and choices?

_____

_____

_____

_____

Can you identify a specific instance where you've silenced your voice to meet the expectations of others?

_____

_____

_____

_____

How can you prioritize your own needs and desires without feeling guilty or selfish? Write three things you can start doing today!

_____

_____

_____

_____

"Unlock a new level of freedom to live your life the way you want."

NELANTHINI RAJESAN

From Mental Bondage to Mental Toughness
by Tony Jones

I had no idea they were aiming at me. The flash of the last gunshot knocked me down. I tried to get up, but my legs would not move. I started praying. Seeing blood spread everywhere, I thought I was about to die.

My friend Jim, who went with me to the block party, swiftly picked me up and put me into the car. In his panic, he ran through a few red lights. I yelled out, "Slow down or you'll crash!"

When we arrived at the hospital, the chaos and commotion broke out in the emergency room. "We need a doctor!" My friends yelled. The nurses seemed shocked, as if they'd never seen that much blood before.

I woke up from intensive care days later and found out I had been shot 8 times and was now paralyzed from the waist down.

The doctor said, "Either that guy couldn't shoot, or God was with you. Not one bullet hit a vital organ." He took a pen from his coat pocket and touched my toes.
"Can you feel that?"

"No," I replied.
"The bullet that hit you shocked your spinal cord. I don't know when you will be able to walk again. It can be tomorrow, next week, or next year...

When I heard those words, I was determined to walk again. I began looking at my toes every day, telling my mind to wiggle my toes. I realized that when those storms come, two things can bring us out of any adversity: effort and attitude.

After a few months, I wiggled my toes. Now I can walk again, and I'm walking out my purpose by helping others get out of jail and stay out of prison.

I invite you to practice mental toughness so you can live your destiny.

Your Turn

Mental toughness is the ability to resist, manage, and overcome doubts, worries, concerns, and circumstances that prevent you from succeeding or performing.

This exercise will help you become mentally tougher than you ever were before, so you can resist and get over every challenge and achieve your financial, fitness, and family dreams, and any other dreams you have.

1. Describe a time when you faced a significant challenge and how you used mental toughness to overcome it:

   _____

   _____

   _____

2. Reflect on the role of mental toughness in achieving your long-term goals and how it can help maintain focus and resilience in the face of setbacks:

   _____

   _____

   _____

3. Describe how mental toughness can be developed and strengthened through daily habits and mindset shifts:

   _____

   _____

   _____

4. Why is developing mental toughness crucial for navigating life's uncertainties and challenges effectively?

   _____

   _____

   _____

5. How does building resilience contribute to personal growth and success in both personal and professional settings?

   _____

   _____

   _____

*"Practice mental toughness so you
can live your destiny."*

TONY JONES

From Emotional Mom to Spirit-Led Mom
by Mirella Acebo

I *hated* myself for not wanting to take care of her anymore. A single mom, an immigrant from Mexico with a 6th-grade education who didn't speak English, she raised me on her own. I never met my dad.

As an adult, I found myself wanting my mom's help, but as an only child, I had become *her* mom instead, as she battled Parkinson's disease, diabetes, high blood pressure, and breast cancer that metastasized into her bones. I was overwhelmed trying to juggle being her caregiver and a new mom: *her* needs with my *own* family's needs. Plus, I felt guilty and selfish for wanting time alone, but I was burnt out.

Then, my mom died, and a whole other wave of emotions took over. I was grieving, lonely, and isolated. The parenting books I read helped a little, but they didn't dive into my *real* struggle— my many internal "mom emotions."

One day, I asked myself: How did the moms of the Bible do it? I saw myself in their stories - loneliness, overwhelm, mom guilt, impatience, and even controlling tendencies —they dealt with it all. God helped me see that my emotions are the most honest thing about me, and I shouldn't hide them or shame them. He taught me to be *real* with how I *feel* so I can *heal* – first with Him and then with others.

Today, I'm a Life Coach, author, and 2x mom, aka the Life Coach Mom, helping other Christian moms through the emotional ups and downs of motherhood. My book connects today's moms to 10 Bible moms they can learn from.

The next time you feel stuck in a "negative" emotion, practice this mantra to give yourself the grace you deserve: Know it. Name it. Share it. Don't Shame it. You're not alone!

Your Turn

Pause for a moment and check in with yourself. Answer these questions:

1. What's one positive emotion you're feeling right now?

    _____

    _____

    _____

    _____

2. What's one difficult emotion you're feeling right now?

    _____

    _____

    _____

    _____

    As you let them in, listen to what they're telling you. Reflect on it below:

    _____

    _____

    _____

    _____

3. Do you hold shame around the way you feel? Or judge yourself for feeling the way you do? Reflect on that below:

    _____

    _____

    _____

    _____

"Know it. Name it. Share it. Don't Shame it"

MIRELLA ACEBO

From Heartbreak to Joy
by Rummana Syeda

I was barely in control of my own body, but I somehow managed to get myself off the floor and into the shower. I woke up from a complete blackout to a version of myself I no longer recognized.

I had mixed substances and went swimming in the pool all by myself, trying to cope with losing my job and with becoming a single mother to my two-year-old son.

The next day, while on a walk, I decided my life needed to change. I had to make peace with my decision to separate from my almost 10-year marriage.

We have to unlearn all the rules of conduct that are not ours, to relearn our core values which are our true beliefs, to silence all outside noise, music, social media, and the approval of our family and friends. To do this, I meditated daily to listen to my inner guidance.

Through my healing journey, I was able to integrate my inner child to actually find pure joy in life. That is when I understood that we must come to a place where we embrace all parts of ourselves. This allowed me to spend countless hours with my son, where I was present with the experience, building core memories for both of us. I became a certified yoga teacher and incorporated dance into my daily life to get out of my mind and get into my body.

My most important transition was becoming an Energetic Healing Coach where I help women create their new world by stepping into their power. It's my mission to help women claim their femininity and find joy in life.

I invite you to listen and accept all parts of yourself so you may integrate them with your current reality and find enchantment in your human experience.

Your Turn

Book a date night with yourself. Light some candles and put on some solfeggio frequencies - they are known to calm the mind and nerves.

Find a comfortable spot to sit with your spine in alignment - that means your sitz bone to the crown of your head is in a straight line.

Close your eyes and start by taking some full deep breaths. Inhale till you feel your belly fill with air and exhale until you have let all the air out. You can count to four for your inhales and count to four for your exhales. Once you feel in tune with your breath allow yourself to breathe in your natural rhythm.

Allow yourself to quietly witness all the chatter - without any judgment, without a need for answers, without the need to correct. Just witness - allow yourself to be the observer.

When you feel ready, allow yourself to feel. Feel whatever comes up for you and give yourself permission to accept all of it.

End this meditation by rubbing your hands together until they warm up, place them over your eyes, then over your heart, and tell yourself out loud: "I accept and embrace all of me."

Write down your experience from this date night for yourself:

_____
_____
_____
_____
_____
_____
_____
_____
_____
_____

"Accept all parts of yourself so you may find enchantment in your human experience."

RUMMANA SYEDA

From Business Breakdown to Leadership Breakthrough
by Carla J. Lewis

Standing alone under the withering glare of 16 angry men, my blood ran cold, and my mouth went dry as I came face-to-face with my professional destiny reflected in their eyes and revealed through their scorn - I was afraid and alone.

On that Monday in September 1979, I was catapulted from the back office of data processing into the center ring of technology's assault on the workplace. Their obvious pain exposed a raw truth to me.

I uncovered a fundamental flaw in changing how people work; it wasn't management's fault. I realized they weren't equipped to navigate transformative change. So I asked, "As we change how people work, don't we also have a responsibility to help them be successful?" This notion was dismissed with a simple reply: "*Carla, we do data, not people.*"

So, I went undercover. Determined to tackle how people can be supported during change, I pursued degrees and certifications in organizational change and development. With grit, tenacity, time, money, and grace from those closest to me, I honed my expertise and developed my superpower: mastering change.

Now, I guide business leaders in navigating change successfully. I help them build trust, manage resistance, and ignite success with strategy and vision. After all, success demands that everyone understands and aligns with both the plans and the desired outcomes from the change itself.

Change is a challenge that affects everyone. Change itself isn't hard; what's hard is letting go of the familiar. Transformation of any size happens only when you feel empowered, competent, and able to embrace the new while thoughtfully letting go of the old.

I encourage you to explore your own change effort, getting clear on the goal and its importance, your commitment, and then engage your support coalition so that you have everything you need to succeed.

Your Turn

Families, communities, small businesses, entrepreneurial ventures, and enterprise shifts are ALL subject to the gravitational pull of "how it's always been" and "the way we've always done it."

Step 1: <u>Clarity.</u> Get crystal clear about the change you want to make and why:

- What do I want to do/achieve?
  _____
  _____

- Why do I want to do it?
  _____
  _____

Step 2: <u>Commitment.</u> What will change and who will be impacted?

- What must I stop, and who will be impacted by my stopping?
  _____
  _____

- What must I start, and who will be impacted by my starting?
  _____
  _____

Step 3: <u>Coalition.</u> Plan the crucial conversations to enlist those who will be impacted. Here are some thought-starters for those conversations:

- I have set a goal to _____
- It's important to me because _____
- There are things I need to start doing and stop doing which can affect you. Specifically,

  By stopping _____, it means I will/won't _____
  By starting _____, it means I will/won't _____

- So, this is what I am asking from you as support for me achieving this goal:
  _____
  _____

You've GOT this!

"Change itself isn't hard; what's hard is letting go of the familiar."

CARLA LEWIS

From Lost to Found
by Todd Krause

I was down on myself and my life. I wanted my life and my struggles with chronic immune deficiencies and autoimmune illnesses to have greater meaning. I was searching for a job, but more importantly, I was searching for myself.

Within two weeks of starting my search, I stumbled upon a listing on a business broker website. The Cleaning Authority in Fishers, Indiana, was available for sale. I purchased this franchise to pay my bills and was determined to grow it.

As I expected, based on my skills and know-how, my business doubled in size in two and a half years and continued to grow. I got to know my Hispanic managers and cleaners on a personal level. They welcomed me into their world with open arms, called me *Jefe*, and said, "You're family now!"

Gradually, I noticed myself making efforts to create a meaningful impact on the lives of my managers, cleaners, and customers, changing their lives for the better.

Looking closer, I discovered that the true impact came from my deep sense of caring for the people around me and their well-being. I found meaning.

I learned how mutually beneficial a strong community inside a business is to the well-being of the world in which it operates. It contributes so much to the growth, health, and purpose of the company.

This discovery led me to a mission to develop community everywhere I can and to teach other business owners to do the same. I empower them to create strong communities within their businesses mutually benefiting them and our society.

Creating strong communities is a win-win-win-win for business owners, employees, customers, and society where they operate.

I invite you to strengthen the community around your business so you can be the positive change your world needs.

Your Turn

First, evaluate the strength of the community inside and outside your business.

Rate the strength of the community of your business:

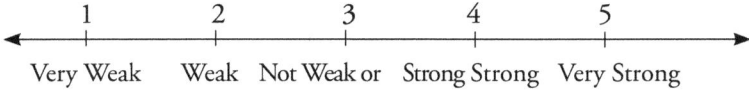

1	2	3	4	5
Very Weak	Weak	Not Weak or	Strong Strong	Very Strong

Inside community rating _____

Outside community rating _____

Then, identify actions you can take to strengthen the community around your business:

- Inside:

  _____
  _____
  _____
  _____

- Outside:

  _____
  _____
  _____
  _____

Take those actions and be the positive change your world needs.

*"We find ourselves when we focus
on our community."*

TODD KRAUSE

From Sorrow to Success
by Ashley Hurjak

I was on my first day of high school, feeling the sting of being excluded. Tennis, my favorite sport, was canceled because no one could access the courts. I decided to join the volleyball team instead—it was the only option available, and I'd played it in middle school.

I met three girls during the first practice, and we connected outside school. However, by the end of that first year, a deep distance grew between us. As the second year began, I faced the pain of their whispers and stares. Eventually, I learned that those same girls were spreading malicious rumors about me. My grades suffered, and I found myself struggling to cope. The betrayal was devastating.

I knew a change was needed. I reached out to the school administration, who took prompt action and validated my feelings. Their support complemented the support of my family, and it was crucial in helping me move forward because this was the environment where I was being hurt.

I learned that experiencing and processing our pain can make us stronger—a strength that helps us thrive in life. By my junior and senior years of high school, my grades dramatically improved, and I was accepted into a top university to double major in biochemistry and applied physics. I even published research in my fields of study.

Now, I'm in college, feeling healed and fulfilled. Inspired by my journey, I started a weekly podcast to share life tools with young people, offering the support I wish I'd had during my hardest moments. Journaling and self-reflection remain central to my growth.

I encourage you to seek out support and reflect on your journey so you can find healing and thrive in your future. Your best days are yet to come.

Your Turn

Take a moment to pause and reflect on your own journey with these questions:

1. What's one memory that challenged you and how did processing it make you stronger?

   _____

   _____

   _____

   _____

2. How have you found support through tough times?

   _____

   _____

   _____

   _____

3. What is one action you can take now to help you thrive?

   _____

   _____

   _____

   _____

"Experiencing and processing our pain can make us stronger."

ASHLEY HURJAK

From Helplessness to Acceptance
by Ruchi Lamba

My heart broke the day my son's teacher told me he might never learn to read. I knew he had autism, but I clung to dreams of a "normal" life for him - graduations, a career, even a family. Her words shattered those dreams and left me feeling helpless.

Nothing prepares you for having a child with special needs. I poured myself into therapies, appointments, and prayers, fighting desperately to change what I couldn't control. But the harder I fought, the more exhausted I became. Then, I discovered the power of *resilient acceptance.*

Resilient acceptance isn't giving up - it's learning to understand rather than change. It began when I chose to observe my son without judgment, focusing on his strengths instead of his struggles.

He loved cooking, so we started making meals together, and through those small moments, I began to see his unique gifts. Slowly, I shifted from resistance to appreciation.

This mindset transformed not just my relationship with my son but my entire life. When I accepted being unemployed, a better opportunity appeared. When I embraced the small size of my dance school, it flourished into a thriving community. Acceptance didn't change my circumstances; it changed *me.*

When life feels overwhelming, perseverance with gratitude can turn pain into power. Acceptance doesn't mean letting go of hope - it means finding strength in *what is* rather than being broken by what isn't.

Try it yourself. Choose one thing you can't control. Observe it without judgment. Don't analyze or resist it - just let it be. Accept it fully, and you'll find its power over you fading, replaced by clarity and calm.

Acceptance is the bridge that transforms pain into power and struggle into strength.

Your Turn

Think about a situation you're struggling with and use the prompts below to practice resilient acceptance.

I cannot control _____

When I observe this situation without judgment, I _____

_____

_____

_____

_____

When I focus on strengths I feel _____

_____

_____

_____

_____

I decide to accept _____
with all my mind, body, and soul.

Now I feel _____

"Acceptance is the bridge that transforms pain into power and struggle into strength."

RUCHI LAMBA

From Secrecy to Freedom
by Margie Simms

I woke up trembling as tears cascaded down the sides of my face. The sudden and firm grip on my husband's arm awoke him. "Margie, what is wrong?!" My only reply was, "God is asking me to tell them what I did!" He knew exactly what I meant.

For many years after that day, God had shown me and directed my path through scripture, church sermons, and even from strangers, so I knew my Heavenly Father would never ask me to do something unless it had an important purpose.

My thought was that I would rather die than ever tell them my secret, but the spiritual death of myself is now what I felt would be my fate.

One Wednesday night, sitting in the pew, I heard that recognizable voice of my Heavenly Parent asking me to break the hearts of my earthly parents. "I need you to tell them, *now!*" The same emotions came flooding back; my husband looked at me. I said, "It's time!"

That weekend, with my knees shaking and my husband by my side, I told my parents that in my senior year of high school, I aborted their first grandchild. Because of their deep love for me, and knowing the pain I had carried for 30 years, the only words they could express were, "We are so sorry!"

God knew I needed all of me healed and whole so I could survive the family tragedies and enjoy the joyous events that were to come.

By a divine appointment, my life path crossed Britt Ivy, and I can proudly say that I am one of the first to graduate from her community, where I deepened my healing.

I invite you to own the secrets that bind you and thrive in the purposes that God has for you.

Your Turn

Do you have secrets that have held you back from the purposes that God has for your life?

_____

_____

_____

_____

Name that secret or secrets:

_____

_____

_____

_____

Who are the people in your life that you could entrust with your secret?

_____

_____

_____

_____

Imagine a life of freedom from bringing your named secrets out of darkness, free from the torture of guilt and shame, and into the light of God, where He wants to heal you. What parts of your life could use a healing touch from your Heavenly Father from the secrets that bind you?

_____

_____

_____

_____

"Own the secrets that bind you and thrive in the purposes that God has for you."

Margie Simms

From Perceived Loss to Promoting Hope
by Lorena P. Frey

The constant fear of finding a military car at home to deliver devastating news was a heavy burden. The Army's motto, "No news is good news," offers little comfort to loved ones.

As the wife of one of the youngest commanders deployed to the Iraq war, due to my experience as a civilian psychotherapist working with military families, I was appointed as the Family Support Group leader. In this role, I coordinated emergency communications through the Red Cross and established the first live birth broadcasts for deployed soldiers.

I supported spouses 24/7, helping them cope with the anxiety and uncertainty of their soldiers' absence.

Three months into the Iraq war, I returned home from a mental break with my kids. I picked up the phone and heard a woman sobbing uncontrollably, saying my husband's name. My heart sank, and my legs buckled; I crawled to shut the door so my children wouldn't hear my cries. I had never shown any emotion before this moment.

I asked, "Did they find his dog tags?" My mind raced, wondering how to tell my kids their hero was dead. Her plea became clear. The news had reported her husband's team was ambushed, and she wanted my husband to find out if it was true. I felt relief when I contacted my husband and heard his voice. The news outlets soon corrected their narratives, too!

My desire to advocate for comprehensive support services for military families before and after deployment increased like never before.

I now speak at conferences, emphasizing the importance of reintegration pathways to ensure they are better prepared and supported throughout the deployment cycle and beyond.

I encourage you to support active military families and retired veterans and their families so you can promote hope when it's most needed.

Your Turn

You can encourage military families to create lasting memories of their loved ones, especially those who may not return home, so we can all help preserve our soldiers' legacy.

Here's a checklist with options so a soldier can engage with their partner or spouse and children while deployed:

1. Record messages, poems, cards, letters, or songs to celebrate your partner or spouse and each child.

    ☐ Today is your birthday. I may not be there physically but …
    ☐ Today is our anniversary and I….
    ☐ It's Mother's/Father's Day and you're the best because…

2. Leave a letter, card, or video to celebrate your child's milestones:

    ☐ Today is the first day of school for you. I wish I were there, but I want you to know…

    ☐ Today is your Graduation…

    ☐ So now you can drive…

    ☐ What! Are you dating? Here is my advice for you…

    ☐ Here's my advice now that you're planning to get married…

    ☐ I can't believe you're having a baby. I remember the first time I held you…

3. Write letters for you as a spouse, partner, etc. Keep them in a box.

    ☐ Write letters for family members so they can read them anytime or on appointed dates.

"The Army's motto, "No news is good news,"
offers little comfort to loved ones."

LORENA P. FREY

From Angry Mom to Calm Mom
by Olivia Bergeron

This was not the mom I wanted to be. I yelled angrily, and my three little children burst into tears. The look in their eyes was devastating.

I was *scary*. I lost it. I felt like a complete failure.

The children were doing the things they did every day: diving into toy boxes and emptying everything onto the floor, asking repeatedly for snacks, and getting into spats.

We were stuck inside for countless hours, and none of them would go down for a nap, so I had no break. When they began shrieking about wanting to play with the same toy, I yelled and put them each in a corner!

I never wanted to see that look on their faces again. I had to learn to be a calm mom for my kids' sake. I decided to become a parent coach and apply what I learned. It worked for me *and* my hundreds of clients.

Using empathy and setting compassionate limits while staying calm helps moms and dads to parent in a way they feel proud of!

I distilled this down into a simple and easy-to-remember framework parents can use, especially when they can feel themselves spiraling.

It's called the Three Ss: stop, soften, see.

Once you recognize you are triggered by your child, you can:
Stop talking or yelling.
Soften your heart towards their child–who will always be your baby!
See your child's point of view.

The outcome of this shift? Seeing your child's point of view makes parenting easier by preventing power struggles allowing you to be a calm mom.

So, every time you find yourself locked in a conflict with your kids, try using this shift. Then you'll see how it will end power struggles, and make family life far more enjoyable–for moms *and* kids.

Your Turn

Replay the last interaction with your child that ended up in a power struggle.

Now imagine the same scenario where you STOP yourself before you yell or get frustrated. What were some points where you could have stopped yourself?

_____

_____

_____

_____

_____

Next, imagine holding your son or daughter in a loving embrace. How do they feel in your arms? Imagine smiling down on them. Feel your heart SOFTEN.

Finally, recount your child's point of view during your last power struggle. SEE where they are coming from, even if you don't agree.

How do you feel now?

_____

_____

_____

_____

_____

I challenge you, for the next five days, to try the Three Ss framework so you can continue to feel this way.

"Ending power struggles makes family life far more enjoyable–for moms and kids."

OLIVIA BERGERON

From Despair to Redemption
by Kristen Matthews Frey

I was afraid to be alone, to shower in my room, or to sleep in my bed. I had trouble sleeping because I had no one to turn to, and I felt alone in a world of authority figures that held power over me.

In 2018, I was deployed overseas and felt honored to serve my country. I was proud to be in the military and loved by my peers as a Preventive Medicine Specialist. It gave me the chance to pursue a career that would promise a future where I could be successful.

Until one morning, a random dorm check turned into a nightmare. A male authority figure came into my room while I was in the shower. As a survivor of childhood sexual abuse, I felt vulnerable, helpless, and violated.

I desperately sought support from the people I chose to sacrifice my life for, and instead (even though what he did was unethical), every day, I was constantly looking over my shoulder in fear of retaliation.

I eventually asked my family and the military police to help guide me through the complaint process against this male predator. No matter how much I followed protocol, nothing was done, and I was made to be the "troublemaker."

Sadly, this is one of the incidents that forced me to prematurely end my military career, and I was diagnosed with severe Post-Traumatic Stress Disorder (PTSD).

My experience has led me to advocate for better measures to protect single soldiers and share how we can overcome sexual harassment and betrayal.

If you are a military survivor of sexual harassment or assault, I encourage you to reach out to support groups like the DoD Safe Helpline and the National Sexual Assault Hotline, so you can receive help and find healing.

Your Turn

Healing from sexual harassment, exploitation, or assault is a deeply personal and non-linear process. Everyone heals differently, and it's important to honor your unique process. What are 3 steps you could take to get through this?

1. _____

2. _____

3. _____

Take small steps, and remember you are not alone in your journey.

How does it make you feel to think about reaching out for help?

_____

_____

_____

_____

_____

_____

_____

_____

If you have not experienced sexual harassment, exploitation, or assault, what are 3 ways you could be there for a friend who has?

1. _____

2. _____

3. _____

"Reach out to support groups so you can find healing and receive help."

KRISTEN MATTHEWS FREY

From Numbness to a Full Life
by Selena Wright

When the doctors told me there was nothing they could do, I was so numbed out to my feelings that it didn't really matter. *I* didn't really matter.

They said Multiple Sclerosis had no cure, and at 25, I would now live a life of deterioration and relapses, getting progressively worse with no hope of ever getting better. Soon there would be the loss of my ability to talk, walk, even think clearly, or remember things. I was not to exert too much energy, especially when I felt tingling or my eyes went blurry as I would only make things worse faster.

A few months after the diagnosis, my mother suggested I go to a personal development center, where I discovered the magic of breathwork.

I dove deep into the experiential workshops and learned how the body talks to us through sensations, and when we don't listen, the blocked energy manifests into pain and symptoms.

My symptoms were my body's way of telling me that I had abandoned it. So, I started feeling and expressing my emotions and stopped numbing myself both emotionally and physically. I decided to speak up for myself and set boundaries so my body didn't have to do it for me through symptoms.

I am more alive and present than ever and my greatest joy in life is supporting others on their healing journey. The doctors were wrong!

Now, as a life and relationship coach, I work with people worldwide who have health and relationship issues, helping them to heal naturally and live from a more joyous, connected, and loving place.

The next time you are experiencing uncomfortable or painful feelings or symptoms, I invite you to slow down and breathe so you can come home to yourself - you are worth it!

Your Turn

Symptoms are the body's way of calling your presence back into it. What is a pain or discomfort you are aware of right now?

_____

_____

_____

Really breathe and tune into that. If your body could talk, what would it be saying to you? What is the emotion you don't want to feel?

_____

_____

_____

If you don't get an answer, just know that by bringing your Breath and presence to that part, it is already starting to heal.

Share your experience here:

_____

_____

_____

It's easy to say "I don't want to feel this pain" and then abandon that part of the body, only to end up on medication to try to take the pain away.

It takes courage to say, "I will breathe, accept this pain, love into this pain, and feel it all, so that I may heal and feel the joy and love that is my birthright."

"Come home to yourself. You are worth it."

SELENA WRIGHT

From Poison to Perspective
by James Marlin

This place was a dump. Greedy little roaches scurried underneath things, and smothering stains covered the cabinets and walls. I had convinced myself it was our little castle, but now I saw the truth. I thought about my 6-year-old son calling this place home. Dropping to my knees, I looked around to get a look from his perspective. I was ashamed and sad for him.

Just 33 days earlier, I had checked into rehab after my father said: "Son, you can be a business owner or a drunk. You can be a husband and father or a drunk. You can be my son or a drunk." The two versions of myself could no longer coexist. Alcohol had poisoned my mind, body, and soul. I thought I was 10 feet tall and bulletproof.

"These people are blowing things out of proportion. They speak of my drinking and know nothing of my thirst," I would say to myself with a smug little grin. In reality, I was 6'2", 125 lbs., shaking, and drinking myself to death.

Newly sober, I saw everything with humility, realizing that certainty is a feeling and feelings are not facts. It taught me that only seeing things from my perspective and avoiding, overlooking, and belittling others' was disastrous.

Now, I speak on stages, encouraging others to value their own perspectives—and those of others. I emphasize the need for respectful communication to build bridges, not drive wedges. We can put disagreement and disrespect back in separate corners, and we can create a livable level of decency that will allow us to coexist effectively.

I invite you to stay willing, respectful, and curious about different perspectives so we can all remain open to a better future.

Your Turn

What beliefs or feelings have you held onto as facts or truths? How has this affected your relationships or decisions? Where has it gotten you in your life?

_____

_____

_____

_____

When have you held onto an idea that others didn't see the same way? How did you react when you realized they saw things differently?

_____

_____

_____

_____

How do you make space for perspectives different from your own? What prevents you from doing so?

_____

_____

_____

_____

*"We need respectful communication
so we are building bridges rather
than driving wedges."*

JAMES MARLIN

From Transformative Shock to Deeper Love
by Jacquie A. McIver

I was standing in the hospital waiting area with a shocked look on my face after my 1-year-old son's second major surgery. My child entered into the world facing serious health challenges, and I had no idea how I was going to care for him.

As tears streamed aggressively down my face, I felt like it was all my fault. A thought entered heavily on my mind: "I am being punished for becoming a parent without being married." Vicariously, I was taught that it is the parent's fault when something happens to their child. Because I heard this belief endorsed and preached at church, these thoughts consumed my mind profusely.

Seconds later, while standing up against the wall, a minister wearing clergy attire walking down the hospital hallway, in what sounded like the loudest voice, said: "This isn't your fault.". It was as if he knew what I was thinking. I realized that God sent an angel to speak to me.

All of the rushing emotions present at the hospital felt like a weight had been lifted off of me. I felt the assurance that everything I face has a greater purpose and that God will get the glory out of our lives. I became clearly aware that God's love would transcend into my heart and help me along this journey.

After this experience, I decided to stop believing the lie that we must earn God's love and that it is based on how well we behave.

Now, I help others who are battling internal negative thoughts and emotions understand and recognize that God loves them, no matter what.

I would encourage you to embrace God's love as a gift so you can see how you will find strength in even the most shocking situations.

Your Turn

Use these 3-steps to transform your life and as a reminder that God loves you no matter what you are thinking or feeling:

1. **Pray** – Write down a prayer below. (A sample prayer: "*Lord, I ask you to help me now and give you my thoughts. I ask you to help me remove negative thinking and give me Your thoughts so I can experience Your love. Thank you for loving me no matter what I face; in Jesus' name, I pray...Amen.*")

    _____

    _____

    _____

2. **Meditate** – Read about God's love. Write what these verses mean to you:

    a. Romans 5:8 -But God showed how much he loved us by having Christ die for us, even though we were sinful. (CEV)

        _____

        _____

    b. 1 John 4:8 - But anyone who does not love does not know God, for God is love. (NLT)

        _____

        _____

    c. 1 John 4:19 - We love because he first loved us. (NIV)

        _____

        _____

3. **Create** a list of words you can declare out of your mouth that confirms that God loves you (i.e., God's love never changes, God's is for me, God is with me, God has a plan for me, etc.)

    _____

    _____

    _____

"Stop believing the lie that we must earn God's love."

JACQUIE MCIVER

From Battles to Boundaries
by Amy Armstrong

I was always on edge, blaming my husband for my unhappiness, trying to cheer him up and win his affection, but he would only talk to the children and not to me. "What are you doing here?" he would ask if I walked into the room. My body held the searing heartache, and all the while I pretended to smile throughout our twenty-five-year charade of a marriage. As I defended him from anyone who would question his status as a family man and provider, I felt like a failure as a wife.

One day, a courageous friend was kind enough to ask me why I said "I'm fine" when I wasn't. "Have you ever told your husband what you expect?" I visibly shook, horrified at the idea of speaking the truth. With her encouragement, little by little, I started to let my voice reveal the real me.

When my husband and children left for a trip, I attended a spiritual retreat where I began sharing my life experience with strangers and listened intently as they shared theirs. The magic of truth-telling washed over me.

I learned to set boundaries and to care for my own needs rather than being dependent on my husband for my well-being. I created a genuine friendship with all the "real" parts of myself and started enjoying my own company.

I now have the joy of helping others create healthy boundaries that safeguard their dignity, worth, and values. I coach parents to address family conflict with authenticity, equality, and responsibility. We uncover new patterns for reducing anxiety, confidently addressing conflict, and celebrating connection.

I invite you to take a step today toward taking ownership of your choices and setting boundaries without blame so you can feel light and free and marvel at your budding new life.

Your Turn

Boundaries are the limit of what we are willing and able to do with our time, money, and energy. Saying what we ARE willing and able to do allows us to set boundaries in a respectful, caring manner.

Think of a situation where you gave in to someone else without caring for your own well-being. Ask yourself these three questions:

1. What is at risk if you tell the truth of what you really need?

    _____

    _____

    _____

    _____

2. How can you show you care without giving more than you really have to give?

    _____

    _____

    _____

    _____

3. How can you give yourself permission to break old habits of being a "pushover"?

    _____

    _____

    _____

    _____

"*Set boundaries without blame,*
so you can feel light and free."

AMY ARMSTRONG

From Burnout to Breakthrough
by Carmen Paredes

I was on a plane from Alaska to Arizona, on my way to have surgery, while bleeding to death from the stomach ulcers I developed trying to climb the corporate ladder. I was overwhelmed with guilt and helplessness because my intention to provide my kids with the life I didn't have resulted in my physical and emotional collapse.

Realizing that my efforts had backfired was a harsh wake-up call. It forced me to reassess my priorities and how I balance work and family life. I finally understood that my children just needed me: happy, healthy, and, most importantly, alive. That's when I decided to begin healing my deepest wounds from the inside out – the ones that made me work myself to almost death to numb my pain and avoid my real feelings.

I researched every possible way to heal the broken parts of me. I started with regular check-ins on my well-being, reflecting on my core values and what truly mattered in my life. This led me to prioritize self-care and re-engineer my daily routines to support a healthier, more balanced lifestyle that aligned with my renewed understanding of success.

Today, I stand on the other side of burnout. I am at peace even through the most difficult challenges. I enjoy a fulfilling life and spending quality time with my kids, and as a professional speaker and best-selling author, I guide driven leaders on how to find balance, avoid burnout, and understand that success is not surviving; success is thriving.

Join me in redefining success as you allow yourself to explore the aspects of your life that may be contributing to stress and burnout. When you prioritize your well-being as much as your professional success, you will thrive in all areas of your life.

Your Turn

Consider these prompts to start your journey away from burnout:

1. Check-In: Use the following scale to rate how you feel when comparing your current lifestyle to your most successful life.

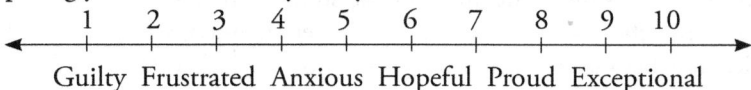

1   2   3   4   5   6   7   8   9   10

← —|——|——|——|——|——|——|——|——|——|— →

Guilty Frustrated Anxious Hopeful Proud Exceptional

2. Reassess your Priorities: List how you're spending your energy throughout the day, identifying what drains you and what energizes you.

_____

_____

_____

3. Circle at least 5 core values that you want to align with as the most successful version of yourself.

Integrity	Respect	Collaboration
Compassion	Excellence	Generosity
Accountability	Transparency	Loyalty
Resilience	Humbleness	Passion
Courage	Gratitude	Curiosity

4. How can your daily activities better reflect your core values?

_____

_____

_____

5. Routine Adjustment: Think of one daily routine that isn't serving you well. Do you really need it? If so, what's one small step you can take to improve it?

_____

_____

_____

"Success is not surviving, success is thriving."

CARMEN PAREDES

From Self-Critical to Self-Love
by Amy Koford

For the millionth time, I observe others around me—trapped in a relentless cycle of comparison, consumed by jealousy and self-doubt. Noticing things about them that I perceive to be better than me, the same old "not good enough" feeling since kindergarten expands inside.

Tears roll down my cheeks as a testament to the daily battle against an unyielding inner critic that drowns out any flicker of self-esteem, kept alive by self-deprecating beliefs that love from God and others was reserved for the perfect. I felt unworthy of the unconditional love I so desperately craved.

As the birth of each of my five babies brought new light, joy, and perspective to my life, I felt a fierce desire blossom within me for them to love and celebrate themselves, to know that they are more than good enough.

My transformation resulted from an extraordinary vision during a session with a hypnotist – a glimpse of my radiant spirit self. She was sparkling with positivity, confidence, and undeniable power, overflowing with love for herself and others.

"Ah, ha! If that's who *I* really am, I can easily love her!" I thought at that moment, accepting my amazing newfound worth. That revelation positively shifted my life.

Self-love and positive self-talk are the keys to upgrading every aspect of our existence.

Motivated by my own transformation, I became a hypnotist, speaker, author, and seminar host. My mission became clear: to guide others to self-awareness and love, helping them break free from the chains of self-criticism.

It's time for you to discover your inner vibrant essence brimming with love and positivity, just waiting to emerge, to create a wonderful ripple effect that is a gift to the world.

Your Turn

1. Imagine you could pull your highest self (spirit) out of your body and place her or him in front of you. What do you imagine your highest self would be like? What positive qualities and attributes do you love about him or her?

    _____

    _____

    _____

    _____

2. Is it easy to love that radiant you? Why?

    _____

    _____

    _____

    _____

    That's who you are and have always been underneath all along! Get to know that magnificent authentic you and it's easier to stop criticizing yourself!

3. Think of a child in your life. What are all the many reasons why you don't want them to criticize themselves?

    _____

    _____

    _____

    _____

    From this moment on, use that same perspective and logic above with yourself.

"You can stop criticizing yourself and connect to your miraculous greatness!"

AMY KOFORD

From Victim to Tigress
by Kanchan Bhaskar

The first time he hit me, my world spun upside down. I was in an arranged marriage to a bright and deceptively charming man who revealed his true nature only after our wedding. I was fearful, numb, lost, and depressed. There had to be a way out.

Growing up in New Delhi's progressive environment, I acquired a unique perception of life: that a woman is an equal partner in a marriage. Marriage meant love, companionship, and caring. A woman was to be respected, honored, and valued—period. My husband did not share these perceptions. I was stuck in a tumultuous, abusive relationship molded by narcissism and alcoholism for far too long.

Belief in self and belief in the Universe can become our weapons of ultimate escape, the foundation for liberation and re-earned dignity. Belief in spirituality provides a new beginning on the path toward the emancipation of mind and soul. With these tools, I built a ramp to climb out of the abyss, little by little, to bring me closer to freedom.

Although I was alone in my fight for survival, I had deep faith in the higher power who presented me with collaborators in the form of angels and mentors to light my way.

My work was slow but steady. Each day was a struggle, yet I remained determined in my single mission to protect my children. I shaped myself into a tigress who could fend for her cubs. Our focus gives us the courage and spirit to keep forging ahead, relentlessly.

Today, a free woman, I'm happily settled, living life on my terms, walking with my head high and chin up.

I invite you to turn into a tigress, a resilient woman, by speaking up so you can tap into the immense strength and courage within and free yourself.

Your Turn

If you are stuck in a toxic relationship, follow this roadmap towards your freedom:

1. Imagine your life free from this toxic relationship. Describe it in detail. This vision is about you and the life you want. Use this image as your compass for the future.

    _____

    _____

    _____

    _____

    _____

    _____

2. Break down the journey to freedom into manageable steps. This might be as simple as reaching out for support, researching resources, creating a safety plan, or building up financial independence. Write these steps down, no matter how small, and take them one by one.

    _____

    _____

    _____

3. Write down a phrase to remind yourself of your strength. This could be something like: "I am worthy of respect," or "I have the power to create a better life."

    _____

    _____

    _____

    Repeat this personal mantra yourself daily as you work toward your freedom. This will rewire your brain and change your mental patterns from negative to positive.

> *"Tap into the immense strength and courage within and free yourself."*
>
> KANCHAN BHASKAR

From Childhood Trauma to Transformation
by Lisa Gunsberg

I kept pressing and asking, "Where's my mom?" At three, I couldn't grasp that she was suddenly gone, and since no one's favorite topic was grief, nobody talked much about her. I grabbed my grandma's leg and stared up at her. Instead of comforting me, she turned away and wouldn't respond to me.

Throughout my childhood, I often rummaged through Dad's drawers, looking for clues about why my mom died.

As years passed, I struggled more and more due to my family's unspoken devotion to silence. In my thirties, a breakup triggered the initial loss, and I realized I'd never grieved. I reflected on how I tried to fill the inexplicable void with food, alcohol, men, and anything else I could jam in there to keep my mind occupied.

I decided to immerse myself in spiritual practices and studied everything from personal transformation techniques to neuroscience. On my path to self-discovery, I started writing a memoir to heal my grief by revisiting the loss of my mom and the impact of my family's silence on every aspect of my life. They inadvertently taught me it was not okay to feel or express my suffering.

I also learned that when we don't communicate our truth, we lack a full sense of our identity. The "fear center" of our brain often doesn't reset after our trauma, and this heightened state of emotion can rule all of our decisions.

This journey has led me to coach people on how to transform their childhood traumas and self-sabotaging behavior into strength and self-empowerment.

I invite you to revisit a hardship or trauma in your life you feel is still unresolved and reflect to allow yourself to grieve. As you start your transformation, get ready to live the empowered life you deserve.

Your Turn

Step 1. Revisit:

Take three deep breaths, and put your hand on your heart. Revisit an unresolved hardship or traumatic event you experienced in your life and write it below:

_____

_____

_____

_____

Step 2. Reflect:

What's the one most important thing you can do now to help you heal and resolve the emotions that stand between you and the empowered life you deserve?

_____

_____

_____

_____

Step 3. Reimagine:

Visualize what your new empowered life looks like and write about how you want to feel as you move forward towards this blessed transformation.

_____

_____

_____

_____

*"When we don't communicate our truth,
we lack a full sense of our identity."*

LISA GUNSBERG

From Trauma to Triumph
by Claudia Lorant

At 15 years old, I sat in my bedroom praying for an end to the nightmare of my father's molestation and attempted rape. My innocence was stolen, and a part of me vanished with it. I called my mom, who was out of the country, but unfortunately, I was silenced.

When my dad came home from work, he put a gun to my head and told me, "Just like I brought you into this world, I can take you out of it."

I stood there in shock, unable to speak or move but crying uncontrollably. At that moment, my spirit left my body, and I floated above while looking down at my dad and me. I wasn't scared in any way. I felt safe and protected, the presence of the Holy Spirit holding me. I don't know how much time passed when, suddenly, I was back in my body.

Defying my cultural rules of being submissive, I screamed at him, "Are you done now?" He lowered the gun, and I ran out the door. This courage was new, and I realized I wasn't alone. I felt strength I never knew I had. I learned that my faith was greater than my fear and God would always protect me.

From that moment on, I developed a profound connection and relationship with God. Now, as a coach, author, and speaker, I share how I prayed and journaled daily to understand my emotions better. Doing this gives us the strength and courage to stand up for ourselves when hurt. We deserve to be loved, safe, and protected.

I invite you to connect with God to find the hope and strength to rise above and no longer let your cultural and traditional upbringing define the woman you were created to be.

Your Turn

1. What is a traumatic experience you would like to overcome?

    _____

    _____

    _____

    _____

2. What is something you would like to say to someone related to
    the trauma you wrote above that you have never felt you have the
    strength to say before? Write it to them below:

    _____

    _____

    _____

    _____

3. How can you develop a better connection to your God so that you
    can feel safe, loved, and protected?

    _____

    _____

    _____

    _____

"Don't let your cultural and traditional upbringing define the woman you were created to be."

CLAUDIA LORANT

From Relinquished to Redefined
by Christina Kopaczewski

"For I hate divorce, says the LORD the GOD of Israel..." (Malachi 2:16, RSV).

This Bible verse held me hostage for thirty-three years. It was a weapon used to silence my pleas for escape during countless times I yearned to break free from an unhealthy marriage.

As my husband's accountability partner, I felt demoralized every time I saw images of women he viewed online. I fiercely guarded his image, sacrificing my mental, emotional, spiritual, and professional well-being so the world would see us as the ideal Christian family. When he was fired as a pastor, we had to move frequently to escape these issues, leaving me utterly isolated, carrying the weight of maintaining appearances wherever we went.

One morning, reflecting on my deep pain, a truth dawned on me: "If we lived in a perfect world, there would be no divorce." God's love, I realized, extended far beyond the confines of an unwholesome marriage. God values us not just as wives and mothers but as individuals deserving security and contentment. This understanding became the cornerstone of my self-worth.

"Be there by 8 am Friday," his email read. A thinly veiled threat disguised as a casual request. "Or else," I felt it implied.

On that Friday morning, at 8 am sharp, I served him divorce papers at the coffee house. It was a symbolic act, reclaiming my power and initiating the journey of rediscovering myself.

This experience taught me a profound lesson I share with the women I coach: you have the power to reclaim your self-worth, rediscover your identity, and redefine your destiny by focusing on what is best for you.

I invite you to practice self-reflection every day so you can regain your strength, rebuild your life, and reclaim your self-worth. You have infinite value!

Your Turn

Employing self-reflection daily will keep you on track toward reclaiming your self-worth, rediscovering your identity, and redefining your destiny. It will get easier each day. You will stand a little taller, and your shoulders will be a little straighter.

Here is where you take back your power in your god-given identity of being created in the image of God to be a reflection of His glory.

As you make these declarations your own and expound on them, you will find yourself empowered to be who you were created to embody.

Daily Declarations:

SELF-WORTH (Genesis 1:26 & Joshua 1:9)

I am beautifully and wonderfully created in the image of God to be a reflection of His glory in everything I say and do.

IDENTITY (John 1:12 & 1 Peter 2:9)

I am who God says I am. I offer love, grace, mercy, justice, and truth to fully embody my identity in Christ.

DESTINY (Romans 8:28 & Ephesians 2:10)

I am a servant leader empowering those around me to be the best version of themselves. I rise by lifting others. I am bold. I am brave. I am kind. I am me.

After reciting these declarations, reflect on them below:

_____
_____
_____
_____
_____
_____

"*Reclaim your self-worth, rediscover your identity, and redefine your destiny.*"

CHRISTINA KOPACZEWSKI

From Shattered Beginnings to Breaking Barriers
by Alinnette Casiano

Arguments, broken plates, the smell of alcohol, and the pain of disappointment filled the empty spaces in my violent childhood home.

Numbing his trauma with alcoholism and drug abuse, my father remained unreliable, leaving severe, invisible scars. Through the tremendous distress, I grew up with the early deception of the "Is this it?" bitter feeling, along with the "you'll never do it" inner voice, the self-doubt, and the nagging sense of inadequacy that comes from always feeling like you don't belong—like you're not good enough.

But faith became my compass when, with shaking hands and a racing heart, I grabbed the college admission letter. I was the first in my family to go to college, all while carrying the weight of helping my family survive financially. I juggled part-time jobs, gained scholarships, and studied through many sleepless nights.

It was not just about getting a degree; it was about breaking the chains of generational struggle and flourishing into who God made me be and not what the world flagged me as I should've been. This led me to choose the right partner to create a family rooted in unity and love.

Now, toward the end of my scholar crusade, pursuing my doctorate, I hold those "freshmen" thoughts close, vulnerable, and hopeful but filled with determination. I now inspire others to understand that self-doubt is the disintegration of self-belief and that they have all they need inside them. I mentor them, create resources, and offer them support. Watching the light of possibility flicker on in their eyes reminds me why it was all worth it.

Let me invite you to throw off the chains of your past. To enable your rebeginning. Allow your deception to become your drive, and your disappointment your victory. You, too, can change your life…if you believe.

Your Turn

Each disappointment is a journey back to a new beginning; when you open to possibilities with grace and faith, you create your own journey of redemption and growth.

Reflect

One of my early deceptions or disappointments is _____

_____

_____

I chose to break the chains of this struggle and enable my rebeginning by _____

_____

_____

Let creativity flow

Draw or write symbols, words, or images to encapsulate your faith and belief.

Reaffirm yourself

Today, I am going to overcome self-doubt by _____

_____

_____

"Allow your deception to become your drive,
and your disappointment your victory."

ALINNETTE CASIANO

From Locked Up to Living Life
by Cheryl Armstrong

I was sixteen years old with a ninety-six-year prison sentence. After driving the car in a tragic crime, I was charged as an adult and now had a dark future ahead of me that held no hope. I was lost in a mindset that had me convinced that life had to be a constant struggle. I was angry and heartbroken and didn't know how to cope with my pain.

While in prison, I found that I had within me a great gift-the power to choose my thoughts in each moment, and, in turn, the quality of my life. I could choose to be happy in an environment designed to oppress me.

Eight years into my incarceration, I began to focus on changing my thinking and re-creating myself. I worked for many years on every aspect of myself, earning a master's degree, getting in good shape physically and mentally, and then helping others to do the same. I created my business and wrote my first book, which I developed into a character development life skills class after my release in 2021.

Now, after spending twenty-six years of my life in prison, I am running this transformative class in numerous prisons and helping individuals face their demons and create a better mindset and future for their lives. I help them see hope and possibility over despair and limitations.

I invite you to embrace the philosophy that no one is their worst mistake, but to be better, we must put in the work to do better.

As you allow yourself to explore the things that are holding you back from being the best version of yourself and own your part in your current reality, you can find a pathway to healing.

Your Turn

Take some time to write and reflect on your worst mistake. The following prompts will aid you in owning your part and forgiving yourself so you can heal and move forward, taking the lessons with you and leaving the pain behind you.

1. Allow yourself to be vulnerable and feel the emotions attached to your worst mistake. What emotions come to the surface for you?

   _____

   _____

   _____

2. What role did you play in this mistake and what do you need to take responsibility for? This is a critical piece of the process that will help you acknowledge the mistake and move forward into growth and lasting change. You do not want to judge or blame here, but take ownership.

   _____

   _____

   _____

3. Think about any unhealthy guilt and shame you may carry around with you as a result of this mistake. Extend some grace to yourself as you look for ways you can learn from mistakes and continually improve yourself. Write your thoughts down to help you process your emotions.

   _____

   _____

   _____

4. How can you work on forgiving yourself for this mistake? As you work on this, it is important to simultaneously practice gratitude, establish healthy boundaries for yourself, and put in the work on the aspects of yourself that led you to this mistake.

   _____

   _____

   _____

"You have within you the transformational power to choose your thoughts in each moment."

CHERYL ARMSTRONG

From Overwhelmed to Confident
by Susan J. Ryan

I was continuously frustrated, overwhelmed, and, yes - sometimes frightened, navigating my caregiving roles for loved ones. No one had answers, and I had no support. My employer didn't have support for caregivers, and I had to maintain this secret to keep my job. I felt like I was on an emotional roller coaster - often blindfolded.

I was afraid I'd do something wrong and didn't know what was right! I began knocking on the doors of my neighbors, giving custom-designed notes about what I was going through, asking if they had any suggestions or knew anyone I could talk with.

I became comfortable being uncomfortable, brave reaching out to people everywhere (except work), and asking for guidance. You can too. More workplaces are now embracing their caregiving team members. Share your journey. Receive help when you need it. Offer help when you can.

I learned we must accept our journey 100% exactly as it is, without the need to like it, agree with it, or even understand it. I eliminated judgment of the situation, myself, or anyone else. Through massive acceptance, I now stay fully present in each moment, confidently making the wisest choices in the most challenging moments and finding joy in the tiniest moments.

As a passionate speaker, coach, author, course creator, and podcaster, I help caregivers learn faster and more easily than I did while knowing they don't ever have to be alone. I help businesses and caregivers work together successfully during their temporary caregiving season so businesses retain their valued employees and both thrive.

If you are a caregiver, please reach out for support. Help is all around. If you don't know who to call, start first with the association for your loved one's diagnosis. You'll soon discover we're all on this journey together.

Your Turn

Create your care support team who's there when you're overwhelmed: Who can you talk with about your feelings *and* your fears?

_____

_____

_____

_____

Who can help you with errands?

_____

_____

_____

_____

Who can watch your loved one for an hour?

_____

_____

_____

_____

Who can be there in an emergency?

_____

_____

_____

_____

"*Massive acceptance and radical presence empower you to meet challenges wisely and embrace life's tiniest joys.*"

SUSAN J. RYAN

From Struggle to Story
by Elayna Fernández

After spending 31 days with these brave transformational storytellers who poured their hearts to show you the path to hope and healing, it is my prayer that their wisdom has brought comfort so you can move forward.

I am grateful for the opportunity to work with each of them as they crafted their individual chapters, and I can assure you they are invested and committed to your healing.

Telling my emotional, vulnerable, raw stories has sustained me over the years because storytelling is a powerful tool to combat shame and trauma and encourage intentional action toward deep personal transformation.

As I celebrated the 20th anniversary of thePositiveMOM.com, I reflected on my dad joking that my school notebooks were "my first blog." I knew my teachers would review my homework, so each day, I wrote a journal entry in the form of a story for them to read. Somehow, I felt more connected to them through this simple, yet brave, ritual. I discovered that I could find meaning, purpose, and relief in storytelling.

When I was seven years old, I started my first storytelling business: a cardboard puppet theater. Soon, I realized that stories do not just entertain - they teach a universal lesson, infuse hope, and bust the cruel myth that people are alone in their hardships and that no one shares their joy.

When you feel unworthy, unloved, or unwell, read a story, tell your story. Use your story as your therapeutic elixir to your present, your link to the past, and your ticket to impact the future.

To be alive is to have a story to tell. I am a storyteller. You are a storyteller. Your life story matters, it's worth telling—and no one can tell it the way you do.

Blessings,

Elayna

"To be alive is to have a story to tell."

ELAYNA FERNÁNDEZ

References

1. Abedi, Sarah. "Motherhood's Hidden Journey: Impact on Maternal Health." *Psychology Today*, 17 July 2024, www.psychologytoday.com/us/blog/healing-the-wounded-healers/202407/motherhoods-hidden-journey-impact-on-maternal-health.

2. Bishop, Adam. "Amygdala Hijack: When Emotion Takes Over." *Healthline*, 15 Apr. 2021, www.healthline.com/health/stress/amygdala-hijack. Accessed 7 Jan. 2025.

3. Cameron, Esther, and Mike Green. *Making Sense of Change Management: A Complete Guide to the Models, Tools and Techniques of Organizational Change*. 6th ed., Kogan Page, 2024.

4. Ely, John T. A. "A Unity of Science, Especially Among Physicists, Is Urgently Needed to End Medicine's Lethal Misdirection." *arXiv*, 2 Mar. 2004, arxiv.org/abs/physics/0403023. Accessed 6 Jan. 2025.

5. Nijjar, Amanda, et al. "The Role of Mindfulness and Meditation in Improving Mental Health in Patients with Chronic Pain: A Systematic Review." *Journal of Pain Research*, vol. 16, 2023, pp. 1561-1574. PubMed Central, https://pmc.ncbi.nlm.nih.gov/articles/PMC10911315/#sec1-8. Accessed 7 Jan. 2025.

6. Society for Human Resource Management (SHRM). "Supporting Employee Caregivers." *SHRM*, www.shrm.org/topics-tools/news/all-things-work/supporting-employee-caregivers. Accessed 7 Jan. 2025.

7. Verplanken, Bas, et al. "Letting Go as an Aspect of Rumination and Its Relationship to Mindfulness and Depressive Symptoms." *Frontiers in Psychology*, vol. 13, 2022, Article 1006445. PubMed Central, doi:10.3389/fpsyg.2022.1006445. Accessed 6 Jan. 2025.

www.ingramcontent.com/pod-product-compliance
Lightning Source LLC
Chambersburg PA
CBHW070124100426
42744CB00010B/1912